ISBN 978-0-282-31715-7
PIBN 10847261

1 MONTH OF
FREE
READING

at
www.ForgottenBooks.com

By purchasing this book you are eligible for one month membership to ForgottenBooks.com, giving you unlimited access to our entire collection of over 1,000,000 titles via our web site and mobile apps.

To claim your free month visit:
www.forgottenbooks.com/free847261

English
Français
Deutsche
Italiano
Español
Português

www.forgottenbooks.com

Mythology Photography **Fiction**
Fishing Christianity **Art** Cooking
Essays Buddhism Freemasonry
Medicine **Biology** Music **Ancient**
Egypt Evolution Carpentry Physics
Dance Geology **Mathematics** Fitness
Shakespeare **Folklore** Yoga Marketing
Confidence Immortality Biographies
Poetry **Psychology** Witchcraft
Electronics Chemistry History **Law**
Accounting **Philosophy** Anthropology
Alchemy Drama Quantum Mechanics
Atheism Sexual Health **Ancient History**
Entrepreneurship Languages Sport
Paleontology Needlework Islam
Metaphysics Investment Archaeology
Parenting Statistics Criminology
Motivational

STATE OF MONTANA

Pioneer Day

November 3, 1911.

ISSUED BY

Department of Public Instruction,

HELENA, MONTANA.

Independent Publishing Co.

Law Relating to Pioneer Day.

1025. That the first Friday of November of each year shall be designated and known as Pioneer Day in the State of Montana.

Act approved, February 26, 1909.

1026. **Exercises in Public Schools.**—That on said Pioneer Day in the public schools the afternoon thereof shall be devoted to the study and discussion of pioneers and pioneer history of the region of country now comprising the State of Montana. (Act approved March 5th, 1903, Sec. 2.) (8th Sess. Chap. 88).)

1027. **Pioneer Medal.**—That the state board of education is hereby authorized to annually award its pioneer medal to the student of the public schools or state institutions who shall on said day deliver the best essay on such subject of pioneer history, having regard to historical research and literary merit. (Act approved March 5th, 1903, Sec. 3). (8th Sess. Chap. 88).

1028. That copies of such essays shall be filed by the said state board of education with the librarian of the historical and miscellaneous department of the state library.

1029. That the Superintendent of Public Instruction shall have power and it shall be his duty to prescribe from year to year a suitable course of exercises to be observed in the public schools of the state on Pioneer Day.

(Approved, February 25, 1911.)

To a Pioneer.

Lay him to rest in the valley he loved,
With its rampart of snow-crowned hills;
Chant softly, ye winds, his funeral dirge,
And weep low, ye mountain rills;
For as free as the mountain air was he
And as pure as the virgin spring
That wells from the rock, in the lofty peaks,
Where the new-forged thunders ring.

No weakling rose plant on his grave,·
Nor a creeping vine sprout there,
But over the head of our stalwart dead
Shall the native pine grow fair.

He blazed the trail and he shaped the State,
He led and we follow his way;
He fought the fight for love of the right
And not for the hypocrite's pay.
As bitter and strong as the North-Wind's blast.
His voice, in censure rung,
And never a traitor betrayed his trust,
But quailed 'neath the lash of his tongue.

No shaft of stone need tell his praise
Nor poet sing of his fame,
For in every breast in the whole wide West
Shall live his honored name.

Lay him to rest in the valley he loved
With its rampart of snow-crowned hills,
Chant softly, ye winds, his funeral dirge,
And weep low, ye mountain rills.
Pillow his head on a lap of cool earth
Where but yesterday he trod,
And there on his couch beneath the blue sky,·
We'll leave him alone with his God.

HELEN FITZGERALD SANDERS

Foreword.

In compliance with Section 1029 which was amended at the last session of the Legislature, the preparation of the Pioneer Day Manual was transferred from the State Historical and Miscellaneous Library to this department.

We have therefore endeavored to publish a few facts relating to the early history of Montana, which we trust will prove interesting and beneficial to the pupils of the state. The manner of observing the day is left to the teacher and the program may be carried out in any way she may prefer.

We trust the day will be fittingly observed, thus carrying out the spirit and intention of the law in creating Pioneer Day.

Superintendent's Letter to Children.

Dear Boys and Girls of Montana:

You are all interested in the great state of Montana whether you were born here or whether you have adopted it as your state. I am sure you are proud of its progress and achievements. It has been a state but twenty-two years and yet in its cities, towns, villages and rural districts it shows material progress that might well be imitated by older states.

We have beautiful churches, commodious, convenient, comfortable, and well equipped school buildings, transcontinental railroads, fine business blocks, rich mines, fertile farms, extensive forests, large lumber and flour mills, and large numbers of cattle, horses, and sheep, and above all we have loyal and patriotic men and women, boys and girls. Today is set apart to commemorate the deeds of those brave pioneer men and women who made it possible to have all the advantages and opportunities that we now enjoy. We are prone to forget in this day of the telephone and the automobile that there was ever the pack horse, the stage coach and the freighter. Many of those old sturdy rugged pioneers have passed from the scene of action. Now and then as we see their faces on wall or canvas, we are reminded that they once lived and played a mighty and important part in the settlement of this country. I advise that each school child look up the life of some pioneer to the end that their deeds may not be forgotten. We now live in safety and comfort in a land of plenty. It was not always thus. Gold was the magnet that drew the early pioneers to Montana. For it he passed through many vicissitudes; for it many gave their lives. How all is changed! Civilization, dear boys and girls, now gives you safety and plenty. I hope you will ever treasure in your memory the heroic struggles of those early pioneers in their desires to bring order out of chaos and the prairie, stream, and mountain to minister to the needs of man.

Very truly yours,

W. E. HARMON,

Superintendent of Public Instruction.

Events Connected With Montana History.

(Chronological Table.)

1803—Louisiana Purchase.

1805—Lewis and Clark discovered the Great Falls of the Missouri.

1863—Gold discovered in Alder Gulch, May 26.

1864—Congress created Montana a separate and distinct territory. Law signed by President Lincoln, May 26.

1864—First Territorial Legislature met in Bannack Dec. 12.
Sidney Edgerton first Territorial Governor.
First Legislature composed of seven councilmen and thirteen representatives.

1865—Capital removed to Virginia City.

1875—Capital removed to Helena.

1876—Battle of the Little Big Horn (Custer's Last Stand), June 25.

1877—Battle of the Big Hole, Aug 9.

1889—Montana admitted into the Union, Nov. 8.
First State Legislature met Nov. 23.
First Governor of the State, Joseph K. Toole.

The First White Men in Montana.

"One of the dreams of the earliest explorers of North America was to cross the continent and find the Western Sea. At first, they believed that it was possible to find some way by which they might sail through to that sea.

Balboa, a Spanish explorer, had crosed the Isthmus of Darien in 1513, and had seen the "Great South Sea" which we now call the Pacific Ocean. His discovery showed that there is a great expanse of water just beyond the land which Columbus believed to be the Indies. A short time later, Magellan, another great explorer, sailed across this ocean and would have circumnavigated the globe but for the fact that he lost his life before the voyage was completed. This exploration showed how great a distance lies between North America and the long sought Indies.

As sailors did not like to go around South America or Africa in order to reach Asia, they tried to find some passage by which they could sail through the American continent. How foolish they were we now know. (Do you know how your country is now trying to solve this problem of a short route to Asia?)

Henry Hudson thought that he had discovered the desired channel when he entered the river which has been named in honor of him. But like the many others who had the same hope, he had found no means of reaching the great ocean which separates America from Asia.

After wide exploration had shown that there was no possibility of sailing through North America to the Western Ocean, the spirit of adventure led many men to attempt the overland trip to the sea. The Spaniards in Mexico were the first to make this trip across the continent.

The French, in the north, had hoped that by sailing up the St. Lawrence they could reach the ocean by sailing through the Great Lakes. The geography of today shows the belief of these early explorers. Just above Montreal there is a stretch of river called La Chine Rapids; that is, "The China Rapids." Whether this name was given in derision or hope, it shows that the St. Lawrence was once thought to be the way to China.

But while the French failed to sail through the continent, they did not give up the attempt to cross simply because of this failure. It was because of their persistence that an adventurous Frenchman was the first white man to tread what is now the state of Montana.

This man, whose name was La Verendrye, was a brave young fellow, the son of one of those hardy pioneers who helped in winning Canada from the savages. More adventurous men than these French Canadians never lived; and young Verendrye and his brother were among the strongest of those brave souls.

As you listen to this story you must keep in mind continually the fact that these explorers were not in search of Montana; for there was then no such name on the map. They were trying to find the great western sea.

Our interests in the Verendryes begins in the year 1728, when the father of the explorers who reached our state was in command of a small post on Lake Nepigon. While at this post he was told by an Indian chief that there was a great lake in the west and that this lake emptied into a river which flowed to the westward. The chief said that he had followed this river until he came to a place where the water ebbed and flowed, but that he was afraid to go further. The Frenchman knew of course, what the Indian did not know: That the ebbing and flowing meant that the ocean was so near that the river was affected by the tide.

As La Verendrye thought over this story told by the chief, he became filled with a great desire to discover this Western Sea. Consequently, he offered to attempt the search if the king would give him one hundred men with a supply of arms, canoes, and provisions. The King, however, was unwilling to bear this expense, but offered La Verendrye a monopoly of the fur trade to the north and west of Lake Superior with the understanding that the work of exploration was to be at La Verendrye's expense. This was the beginning of the search that led two of his sons into what is now the state of Montana.

La Verendrye used the fur trade to induce several other men to help him in his great work; but the expense was so great that he had to make larger promises than he could fulfill. Later, this brought disaster to him. In 1738 he had raised money enough to enable him to begin his journey.

In this day of railways and good roads, it is hard to appreciate the difficulties that Verendrye met. In the first place, there were no roads whatever. The best method of travel was by water wherever that was possible. But even where there were waterways, the explorer was handicapped by the fact that the courses of the rivers and the extent of the lakes were unknown. The distance which La Verendrye was to cover was very great, almost too great for a party with such equipment as he could provide.

Furthermore, the Indians were often hostile. The eldest son of La Verendrye was killed by the Sioux as he was attempting to return from the first expedition made in search of the Western Sea. Even where the Red Men were not unfriendly they could not aid very much because they themselves were very ignorant of the country except in that region where they had their hunting grounds.

Another difficulty was in the mutiny of men who made up the party. After they had gone a certain distance on the first trip, they refused to go further, thus making a heavy expense without returning any gain. This was very hard for La Verendrye to bear, because he had very little money and every item of expense meant a great deal to him.

It was very hard for La Verendrye to get money for his purpose. Two or three times the King refused to give aid, even though he was told that if he would give six thousand dollars the enterprise would be successful. But to the King, finding the Pacific was not worth as much as six thousand dollars.

For several years La Verendrye worked with all his might to make his plan a success. He built several forts and established a large trade with the Indians; but he was never able to get any money from the government for the purpose of aiding his great enterprise. The King's greatest concession was that La Verendrye might rent his forts to other traders and thus get money to equip an expedition to search for the Pacific.

By the latter part of the year 1738, he had reached the country of the Mandans, that is, what is now North and South Dakota. But the Indians stole his presents; and his interpreter fell so deeply in love with an Indian girl that he ran away in pursuit of her. Under such circumstances as these, it was useless to remain with the Mandans. Consequently La Verendrye left two men to learn the language of the Indians and set out upon his return to Fort La Reine, a post which he established on the Assiniboin River.

This trip was so severe that La Verendrye was almost broken down. Therefore he no longer sought to find the Pacific himself, but turned the work over to his two sons Pierre and the Chevalier. These brothers were probably the first white men to set foot on the soil of what is now Montana.

During the years 1739, 1740, and 1741, these brothers were on the alert for news of the Western Ocean. Indeed, Pierre, the elder of the brothers, having heard of some Indians who lived toward the sunset, in country where white men lived, set out to find these Indians. From the Indian chief he learned that these white men wore beards, that they prayed to the Master of Life, that their houses stood near a great lake, and, most marvelous of all, the water of this lake ebbed and flowed and was not good to drink.

This statement made Pierre de la Verendrye believe that these Indians had been among the Spaniards who were living near the Pacific Ocean, perhaps in California. Eager to find that ocean, he set out with two men on the search. He expected to be able to hire guides of the Mandans (in what is now Dakota); but none could be obtained. Dissappointed in this, he was compelled to return to his father and brother at Fort La Reine.

This failure, however, did not dishearten the Verendryes; but the next year (1742), Pierre and his brother, the Chevalier, set out to accomplish the work that Pierre had failed to do. They left Fort La Reine in the latter part of April, 1742, expecting to go again to the Mandans and to proced from that country to the land of which the Indians had told them,— the land near the great lake whose waters ebbed and flowed.

As this is the expedition in which the first white men came to Montana, we can afford to trace the route of the explorers with care. It seems probable that they ascended the Assiniboin River to the mouth of the Mouse River; then they went up that river as far as possible; and finally traveled overland to the country of the Mandans. Perhaps they found that tribe near the Heart River, or the Cannon Ball, near the present site of Bismarck, North Dakota.

The Mandans were very glad to see them. Indeed they were

so veryglad that they feasted their white visitors almost past all endurance. The Indians provided also quite a variety of of entertainments for their guests. There were archery contests among the boys. The men who had horses held a series of races. The old Indian game of stick and the rolling ring was played a great deal.

All this might have been pleasant enough to the Verendrye brothers if they had not had serious work in view. They inquired continually in regard to the Horse Indians, whom they expected to lead them to the Western Sea. But the Mandans knew very little of the Horse Indians. Indeed, they did not so much as know where they lived; but they were expecting a visit from that tribe. The Verendryes waited as patiently as they could until late in the summer. They then decided that they would go in search of the Horse tribe.

With two Mandans whom they had hired as guides, they set out from the scene of their long visit. Their equipment was made up of a few saddle horses, some pack animals, a stock of presents for the Indians, and such baggage as seemed absolutely necessary. Their course was to the west-southwest, with the Missouri River on their right and the Black Hills on their left.

Day after day, they traveled across rolling prairie well covered with grass, but poorly supplied with timber except along the streams. They saw "earths of different color, blue green, red, or black, white as chalk, or yellowish like ochre." This must have been in the "Bad Lands" of the Little Missouri.

After they had traveled about three weeks they came into a group of hills, which perhaps form a part of the Powder River Range. Here they expected to find the Horse Indians. They built a cabin and resolved to wait for the tribe to come. Every day they kept fires to attract the attention of anyone who might be near. And often they would climb to the tops of the highest hills in the hope of seeing the long sought Horse Indians. It seems very likely that this camp was in what is now called south-eastern Montana:

For more than a month they waited. Finally, about the middle of September, they saw smoke on the prairie at some distance from them. They thought that they had at last found the tribe for whom they had been waiting. But in this they were disap-

. pointed. They found that these Indians were of a tribe called Beaux Hommes, that is, Handsome Men. They were probably Crow Indians.

The lack of an interpreter made it impossible to talk much with the Crows. Still by means of signs, the white men made it known that they wished to find the Horse Indians. Some presents persuaded the Handsome Men to offer two of their young warriors as guides. With these, the Frenchmen found the Horse Indians.

If the Verendryes hoped to learn about the Pacific from the the Horse Indians, they were very deeply disappointed; for no one of that tribe had ever seen the ocean.

Their knowledge was all second hand. They had heard of the ocean from the Bow Indians. To this tribe, the Horse Indions offered to lead the party. But the offer came only after a great many presents had been given.

To the southwest the party then proceeded for several days, coming at length to the Bow Indians. This tribe was probably a band of western Sioux. They were quite like the Mandans, the Crows, and the Horse Indians in their ignorance of the Western Sea. But they had heard of that great lake from captives taken in war. Perhaps these captives were of the Snake tribe..

The Frenchmen found that the Bow Indians were going to send out a very large war party against the Snakes. The Verendryes believed that by going with the Indians they could reach the Pacific. Indeed, the Indians told them that they were going to the mountains from which it was possible to see the ocean. The expedition proceeded to the southwest and finally reached the Shining Mountains, that is, probably, the Big Horn Range in Wyoming. The Chevalier, who had left his brother behind, to watch over the baggage of the party, was very eager to climb the mountains. He believed that from their summit he could see the waters of the Pacific. He would have had to have keen eyes to see across the thousand miles between those mountains and the ocean!

The war party broke up in a panic. Because of this, La Verendrye was unable to climb the mountains. He returned with the Indians to the place where he left his brother. The whole party then moved toward the east-southeast. The Frenchmen left the Bow Indians about the middle of March,

1743, and continued toward the east until they again reached the Missouri. Up this river they then continued their course, reaching the Mandans in May.

It is in connection with the Shining Mountains that a very serious mistake has been made in telling the history of Montana.

An early writer wrongly described the course of the Verendryes as being up the Missouri from the villages of the Mandans. Because of this, it was believed that the explorers must have reached the mountains somewhere near Helena and that the Shining Mountains were the Montana Rockies.

Although this writer discovered his mistake and corrected it, many people continued to believe that the Verendryes had seen the Gates of the Mountains and the Bear's Tooth near Helena. This is, of course, a mistake; for the Verendryes left the Missouri somewhere near Bismarck, North Dakota, and traveled to the southwest. Consequently, the only part of Montana which they saw was the southeast corner.

A part of the story of the Verendryes is that, after reaching the Missouri for the second time, they planted a leaden plate beneath a pile of stone upon a high hill overlooking the river. Upon the plate was engraved the coat of arms of the King of France.

A few years ago, L. M. Corson, who was then very much interested in the history of Montana, believing the mistaken account of the trip up the Missouri, thought that he had discovered the mound upon which the leaden plate had been buried. After patient investigation, however, he was forced to the belief that the Verendryes did not see the mountains near Helena, that they did not travel over very much of the present state of Montana, but that they crossed only the southeastern corner of the state.

Here then seems to be the truth in this famous story of the First White Men in Montana. They were indeed in our state; but their stay was very brief; and what they saw was very limited. While their purpose was like that of Lewis and Clark, to cross the continent and reach the Western Ocean, their work was a failure and they cannot be given the prominent place in Montana history that was once given them.

After their return to Canada, they lost almost all their possessions. Of this, the elder brother said: "We spent our youth and property in building up establishments so valuable to Canada; and after all, we are doomed to see a stranger gather the fruit we had taken such pains to plant." The goods which they had left at the trading posts were wasted; their provisions were consumed; and even the men in their pay were used to do the work of others.

As the story is told by Parkman, the brothers sank into poverty and neglect. Their services were unrewarded. After Canada passed from the French to the English, the Chevalier de la Verendrye, one of the first white men to see the Rocky Mountains in the north, perished in a shipwreck off the coast of Cape Breton, in November, 1761."—C. L. Robins.

The Revenge of Rain-in-the Face.

In that desolate land and lone,
Where the Big Horn and Yellowstone
  Roar down their mountain path,
By their fires the Sioux chiefs
Muttered their woes and griefs.
  And the menace of their wrath.

"Revenge!" cried Rain-in-the-Face,
"Revenge upon all the race
  Of the White Chief with yellow hair!
And the mountains dark and high
From their crags re-echoed the cry
  Of his anger and despair.

In the meadow, spreading wide
By woodland and riverside
  The Indian village stood;
All was silent as a dream,
Save the rushing of the stream
  And the blue-jay in the wood.

In his war paint and his beads,
Like a bison among the reeds,
  In ambush the Sitting Bull
Lay with three hundred thousand braves
Crouched in the clefts and caves,
  Savage, unmerciful!

Into the fatal snare
The White Chief with yellow hair
  And his three hundred men
Dashed headlong, sword in hand;
But of that gallant band
  Not one returned again.

The sudden darkness of death
Overwhelmed them like a breath
  And smoke of a furnace fire:
By the river's bank, and between
The rocks of the ravine,
  They lay in their bloody attire.

But the foemen fled in the night,
And Rain-in-the-Face, in his flight,
  Uplifted high in air
As a ghastly trophy, bore
The brave heart, that beat no more,
  Of the White Chief with yellow hair.

Where was the right and the wrong?
Sing it, O funeral song,
  With a voice that is full of tears,
And say that our broken faith
Wrought all this ruin and scathe,
  In the year of a Hundred Years.
        —Henry Wadsworth Longfellow.

First Steps in Civilization.

It is not very long since Montana acquired her first institutions of civilization. California and Oregon were earlier in settlement and in the introduction of modern civilized ways of life and establishments. The mountainous nature of the country, the lack of easy means of travel and transportation and the hostile Indians held the Rocky Mountain district back. The first printing press did not reach the state 'till 1863. It was brought to Bannack by Benjamin R. Dittes and D. W. Tilton, both well known early neswpaper men. Together they published the "Newsletter." In August, 1864, the second neswpaper, "The Weekly Montana Post," made its first appearance. It was published at Virginia City. The "Montana Democrat" soon followed it in the same town, and the fourth paper, "The Helena Herald," was established at Helena in 1866.

While religion was first introduced into Montana by the Catholic priests, the first Protestant sermon was preached within the limits of Montana territory by a colored Methodist preacher at Bannack in 1862. His name is forgotten. Fathers DeSmet and Ravalli were among the most notable of the early Catholic missionaries within this territory. Protestant missionaries passed through Montana on their way to Oregon, as early as the thirties, and some of them doubtless held services and preached sermons within the borders of the present state. Accounts of such occurrences are to be found in the life of Col. Joseph L. Meek, and in other historical works dealing with the Rocky Mountain region, but that was in the days when this was part of the Louisiana purchase, long before it even became a part of Missouri territory.

It was in 1864, that Helena was christened, and other camps in Lewis and Clark county, then known as Edgerton county in honor of the first territorial governor, were established before this, the first county seat being Silver City. The first Sunday school at Helena was located in a large log building on Joliet street, and the teacher was a Mr. McLaughlin. Mr. Reinig's store was opposite the log Sunday school, as was the early home of Thomas C. Groshan, a well known resident of Helena for years. The first public school located at Helena according to the records, was opened in 1867. It was a log cabin on the ground which is now occupied by the residence of H. M. Parchen. The school teacher was a minister, Mr. Campbell. Prof. Dimsdale, whose book tells early incidents of the territory, as the first school teacher at Virginia City, where he taught school in 1864. Judge Cornelius Hedges was the first lawyer to hang out a shingle at Helena. He walked almost the entire distance from Virginia City to Helena in January, 1865, and opened a law office here. Mr. Word was the first sheriff and Orison Miles the original justice of the peace. One of the first professional acts of Judge Hedges as a lawyer was to draft the will of Johnny Keene, who was among the first group of road agents to be hanged on this side of the mountains.—Montana Lookout.

Echoes From Early Days.

The Pioneers.

Long and weary was the journey
As our fathers crossed the plains;
Many walked, though sick and ailing,
Many walked through drenching rains.
Crossing rivers, rounding mountains,
Which like mighty giants stood;
On the banks of clear, cool waters
Did they eat their share so good.
As along through gorgeous canyons,
Waiting for the end to come,
They traveled steadily onward
To reach the valley and their home.
Their yearning eyes and dear brave
    hearts,
Were met by far-stretching land;
And many times a hostile tribe
Attacked this fearless band.
Still they pressed on until they came
To a stream so clear and sweet,
They tilled the soil and farms were made
And corn grew at their feet.
And from the mountains, logs were
    brought,
And sun dried bricks they made;
From these two things their homes they
    built
And in this valley stayed.

—MAY HOOD.

Montana's First Christmas and Those Who Participated.

"On Christmas day, 1832, was celebrated one of the first holidays of the kind in the Northwest. Just across the line in Idaho, Captain Bonneville's party of trappers, hunters and pioneers had gone into their winter quarters. And they had earned their right to celebrate. Since May of that year they had toiled their way up the Platte across Wyoming and over the mountain; they had fought Indians and suffered hardships and were prepared to enjoy their rest in winter quarters among the friendly Nez Perce. Rude cabins of logs were erected, together with a large barn for the horses, and the whole was surrounded with a palisade as a protection against hostile Indians. A short distance away were the lodges of the Nez Perces.

These hardy sons of the plains and forest did not forget Christmas, although thousands of miles from civilization. On Christmas eve the festivities began with rude fetes and rejoicing. The lodge of the Nez Perce chief was surrounded and in lieu of Christmas carols he was saluted with discharges of musketry. The old chief was highly flattered and invited the whole company to a feast on the following day. It was the first recorded Christmas in an Indian wigwam. And it goes without saying that it was highly enjoyed. Skins were placed on the ground and upon these was placed abundance of venison, elk and other game. There was a short prayer and then the entire company seated themselves Turkish fashion and pitched into the feast. This followed by a long series of games, running, jumping, wrestling, shooting at the mark and the like—between whites and Indians.

The men who made up this party of hardy adventures are worthy of more than passing note. They are the path breakers, the vanguard of civilization. They constitute a type the world will never see again; a type long passed away. The free-hunter, the free-trapper, the Indian trader, and the pack-horse man were the original explorers of Montana and the West. Men like Sublet, Bridger, McKenzie, Liver-Eating Johnson, Culbertson, Coulter, Malcolm, Clarke and a hundred others are the heroes of a wonderful romance, the half of which has never been told. On that Christmas day in 1832, in Captain Bonneville's camp, their types were all represented.

Foremost of all these was the free-trapper. When frequently

connecting themselves with large hunting parties they gloried in their independence. They provided their own horses, guns and equipment; hunted, trapped and traded on their own account, and disposed of their pelts to the highest bidder. With withering contempt they looked down on the hired trappers who were outfitted by the traders.

"Constant contact with the wilderness and savage conditions made them discard, as a matter of vanity, every suggestion of civilized life. In manners, habits and dress they followed the Indian. To mistake a free-trapper for an Indian was the greatest compliment that could be paid him. He permitted his hair to grow to great length. Sometimes it hung carelessly over his shoulders, frequently it was carefully coombed, plaited and tied up with brilliant colored ribbons. A hunting shirt of colored calico, or of ornamented leather, fell to the knee. His leggings were curiously fashioned and decorated with strings and fringe, and hawk's bills. His moccasins were always of the finest Indian fabric and properly decorated. Over his shoulders he flung a blanket of scarlet, fastened with a red sash around his waist in which he carried his pistols, knife and Indian pipe. And his savage vanity extended to his gun and horse. The former was as a general thing lavishly decorated with brass tacks and vermillion. The horse was the pride of the trapper and it was caparisoned in the most dashing and fantastic style. The bridles and crupper were weightedly embossed with beads and cockades, and the head, mane and tail were interwoven with an abundance of eagles' plumes fluttering in the wind. Then the animal was streaked and spotted with vermillion and white clay. This was his gala attire and in it he was ready for revels, fighting or love-making.

"Such were some of the old Montana types, and such were the men who on Christmas day, 1832, gathered around the yule log in Captain Bonneville's camp."

Establishing Missions.

(By Charles Schafft—Written in 1867).

In 1840 Father De Smet, a missionary of the Society of Jesus, made his first appearance in the Rocky Mountains to convert to the faith of the Cross the Red Men who heretofore had only seen small rays from the great lights of Christianity reflected from a few Canadian voyagers or Iroquois! Indians that frequented the country for the purposes of trapping and trading for furs.

The Flatheads, inhabiting the Bitter Root valley, were anxious to try the new trail, which promised immortality to all' who followed its windings, and repeated messages were sent by them to St. Louis for a priest, or as they term it, a "Blackgown." One of these convoys consisted of five or six Indians and a Protestant clergyman (who accompanied them to go on some distant mission of his own) were all murdered (except the clergyman) on their return from St. Louis by a party of Sioux who mistook their nationality and believed them to be enemies.

Catholic priests were not very plenty in those days, and it was only upon a final effort on the part of the Flatheads, that the Superior of the Jesuits in St. Louis, felt himself called upon to send a teacher.

Father DeSmet was chosen for the perilous task of carrying the cross to an unknown wilderness and teaching its symbolical meanings an efficacy to the nations of red men dwelling in the mountains. With the true spirit of the Jesuits of old, who enriched the soil of Canada with their blood, the young father started to his new field alone. The principal part of his journey lay along the great Missouri, but the Flatheads knew of his coming, and at a considerable distance from their village he was received by a delegation of the tribe, who escorted him in triumph to the Bitter Root Valley.

The Father found here in the elevated regions of the mountains a fine country with soil sufficiently rich to produce all that a husbandman need require; timber, grass, and water were abundant, and could not be excelled anywhere. The people whom he came to instruct looked as yet kindly upon the faces of white men, with whose vices they were unacquainted. He found them ready and willing to be taught, and after the principal features of the Catholic religion had by means of an interpreter, been impressed upon their minds, the chiefs and head men came forward to be baptized. These Indians as well as the neighboring tribes had always practiced polygamy, and the sincerity of their conversion was proven by their readily resigning all extra wives and becoming united to only one, in accordance with the articles of their adopted faith.

Like all other Indians they had heretofore believed in the Happy Hunting Grounds, and in a Great Spirit, who, assisted by a lesser one, governed and ruled the universe, and from whom came all good. They also believed in the existence of bad spirits, who ruled over disease and destruction, and in order to propitiate these latter in cases of sickness or impending evil, the usual "Medicine" grounds abandoned throughout the country and propitiatory offerings, consisting of beads, tobacco, etc., were hung on peculiar trees or laid on certain rocks, to incline the spirit (who it was supposed, held in such places their residence), to give them success on the warpath, hunting excursions, or any other important undertaking.

Even at this day, some of the most prominent Indians, among whom is Victor, head of the Flathead nation, believe in the existence of a Lake, said to be located somewhere between the country of the Upper Pend 'Oreilles and Kootenais, which Lake they maintain is inhabited by all kinds of animals, such as buffalo, elk, deer, etc., that live and thrive under the waters of the Lake, and a very large beaver is the presiding genius over the submarine assemblage. Victor, the above mentioned chief, says that he has seen the lake with his own eyes, and offered last fall to take one of our distinguished officials to the spot. However, the season was too far advanced, and the project of visiting this Barnumian spot was deferred until next spring. A tradition is current among these Indians of a great flood that at one time covered all the earth; but that a very large beaver was saved from the general destruction. The beaver was always looked upon by them as an intelligent and superior animal. They used to say, "We are like the beaver, but a little above him; for he builds houses as we do, but unlike us he cannot pull them down again."

Father De Smet on his first visit tarried only long enough in the mountains to see that the seeds sown by him were not cast upon a barren soil, and then returned to St. Louis to report progress and obtain assistance. He returned in 1842, accompanied by Fathers Point and Mengarini, together with several lay brothers and a regular missionary establishment was begun in the Bitter Root valley under the name and title of St. Mary's Mission.

Agriculture at this time was yet unknown in the Rocky Mountains. The Indians, indeed, were accustomed to rip open the soil, but it was in search of camas and other esculent roots. The missionaries, provided with an assortment of seeds, and the most indispensible agricultural implements, opened now the "first farm in Montana" and began to test to the Indians and half-breeds the benefits to be derived from the culture of the soil. That their time and labors were not lost, is well proven by the fine farms which the Flatheads possess in the Bitter Root valley at the present time.

Steps were now taken to multiply the missions in order to facilitate the spreading of the faith among the neighboring tribes. That of the Couer d'Alenes was established under Fathers Point and Hoeken in 1844. (This year brought also a reinforcement with the return of Father DeSmet of several other Fathers and lay-brothers; among the number were the well known Father Louis Vercruyssen and that noted physician Father Ravalli). The same year under the care and superintendence of Father Ravalli, a chapel was built at Colville. The old St. Ignatius Mission, among the Kalispells, about thirty miles from Colville was established in 1845, and was transferred in 1859 by Father Hoeken to the Sonielem valley, now a part of the general Flathead Reserve, among the upper Pen d'Oreilles, and a site was here chosen which cannot be excelled either in a practical view or for scenic beauty in Montana.

Pioneer Days.

O Memory, thy pictures are vivid and grand;
I see-in thy gallery a used-to-be land
Where many prospectors fearless and bold,
Had settled out west in their fever for gold;
And in fancy I see in that dim far away
Those faces of friends in the Pioneer day.

I see a log-cabin with chinking daubed o'er
But the latch-string hangs out on that rude cabin door---
A welcome to strangers to share the pine-knot,
And list to the yarns, now long since forgot.
Oh, hearty the hand shake and gladsome the gaze,
When we welcomed a stranger in Pioneer days.

And music! I fancy again I can hear
The old fiddler's tuning as midnight draws near;
And I see the sweet blushes of Tracy's bride, when
She must choose for a partner one man out of ten.
And merry the dance 'till the sun's slanting rays
Peeped over the hilltops in Pioneer days.

I see the cold stars hanging high in the sky
As they winked and they blinked when my comrade and I
Lie rolled in our blankets on some mountain slope
Where we'd prospected day after day, filled with hope;
And the coyote's lone howl seemed in dreamland's fair maze
Like a soft lullaby—in Pioneer days.

O, Pioneer days so wild and so free,
The memory of you brings sweet rapture to me.
And the friends I once loved—some are dead—and they say
Some are spending life's winter in lands far away;
But wherever they are, do they still sing the praise.
Of life in the Rockies in Pioneer days?

—GOODYEAR LANSING.